I0140468

FAT POETS SPEAK

VOICES OF THE FAT POETS' SOCIETY

FRANNIE ZELLMAN, EDITOR

KATHY BARRON, ANNE S. KAPLAN,
CORINNA MAKRIS, LESLEIGH J. OWEN
& FRANNIE ZELLMAN

PEARLSONG PRESS
NASHVILLE, TN

Pearlsong Press • P.O. Box 58065 • Nashville, TN 37205
www.pearlsong.com • www.pearlsongpress.com

"Priorities," "Fat Bitch," "No Reason to Feel," "Feast of Fruit," "No Magic
Pill for Me" ©2006 Kathy Barron • "My Vulgar Love," "Used to be a Nice
Girl," "Yummy Fat Love," "Shame Doesn't Live Here Anymore" ©2007
Kathy Barron • "RAPUNZEL Revisited" ©2006 Anne S. Kaplan • "Turning
Point" ©2006, 2007 Anne S. Kaplan • "I Am Mother Earth" ©2006
Corinna Makris • "I Celebrate My Every Curve" ©2007 Corinna Makris •
"Ode to My Upper Arms," "En Vogue," "Fat Beauty," "Ceres," "Venus Envy,"
"Mirror, Mirror," "Mirror, Mirror, Part 2," "no one's Gaia" ©2006 Lesleigh J.
Owen • "Half," "Arctic New Year" ©2007 Lesleigh J. Owen • "I Sing the Fat
Self," "Big Fat Bitch," "To My Grandma Helen," "Freezing in the Sun," "Did
You Lose Weight? 1, 2 & 3," "Making Movies" ©2006 Frannie Zellman
All other material © 2009 by Kathy Barron, Anne S. Kaplan, Corinna
Makris, Lesleigh J. Owen, & Frannie Zellman

The Fat Poets' Society is donating the royalties from this book to the
National Association to Advance Fat Acceptance (NAAFA).
For more information on NAAFA, see www.naafa.org.

ISBN-10: 1597190160 • ISBN-13: 9781597190169

Book & cover design by Zelda Pudding

No part of this book may be reproduced, stored in or introduced into a
retrieval system, or transmitted, in any form or by any means (electronic,
mechanical, photocopying, recording, or otherwise), without the written
permission of the publisher, with the except of brief quotations included in
reviews.

Quantity discounts are available to your business, institution or organization
for reselling, gifts, fundraising or educational purposes, or incentives.
For more information contact Pearlsong Press • P.O. Box 58065
Nashville, TN 37205 • 615-356-5188 • sales@pearlsong.com

Library of Congress Cataloging-in-Publication data

Fat poets speak : voices of the fat poets' society / Frannie Zellman, editor.
    p. cm.
ISBN 978-1-59719-016-9 (original trade pbk. : alk. paper)
 1. American poetry—Women authors. 2. Overweight persons—Poetry. I.
Zellman, Frannie, 1954–
PS589.F38 2009
811'.60803561—dc22

                                                    2008041658

To the fat activists who have gone before us
and the fat activists who will come after us,
to the fat activists who stand beside us
and to all of the fat people whose voices
have not been heard.

To all of the fat people who live among us
but haven't yet learned how to fight back—
this is for you.

And with gratitude and love to Mary Ray Worley,
proud fat activist and friend,
who initiated and inspired
the Fat Poets' Society.

INTRODUCTION

There are now numerous blogs devoted to the idea that fat people should not only accept themselves, but liberate themselves from thin supremacy, the idea that thin people are somehow better and deserve to rule over fat people.

But there are still very few places on the Net or in real life where fat people can write and share poetry that speaks to their lives and concerns and wishes. Partly with this in mind, NAAFA—the National Association to Advance Fat Acceptance—held the first workshop devoted to "Fat Poetry" at its yearly convention in July 2006. Those who participated were made members of the Fat Poets' Society (FPS).

It is difficult for me even to try to explain how liberating and exhilarating it was to talk with poets about writing poetry that spoke to the issues and concerns we have as fat people in a thin-centric society. But it was twice as exhilarating to write with them as we all looked within ourselves and around and about to produce poems that spoke to our fat selves.

I have written poetry since the age of six, but somehow felt that I was writing in a dream before I realized less than ten years ago that I had never been centered as a poet because I had never been able to write about my own body and feelings as a fat person.

In this book you will meet us: five fat poets writing about our hopes, despair, happiness, sensuality, dreams, hurts, healing, exhilaration—about what it is to be alive and fat in a world that hates fat people, but in which we somehow persevere to make ourselves heard and ultimately celebrate.

We, members of the Fat Poets' Society, are Kathy Barron, Anne Kaplan, Lesleigh Owen, Corinna Makris and Frannie Zellman. Welcome to our world.

Our biographies are at the end of the book.

Frannie Zellman
Editor

"Did you lose weight?"
"No, it was stolen."

Lesleigh J. Owen

"Did you gain weight?"
"Why? Do I look even more wonderfully round than before?"

Kathy Barron

CONTENTS

PART I

SINGING THE FAT SELF

I Sing The Fat Self
(To the memory of Walt Whitman)

I sing the fat self that flourishes, acquires girth,
births and blooms its stomach and thighs and limbs,
soft but sturdy as it flows among people and
things it knows and greets. I sing the self that bounces,
plump and easy and free, not tightened or wired
or cut like meat into the correct sizes for freezing and eating. I
sing the self that hugs and is hugged, is cuddled in all places,
sleeps and slips sweetly against its loving partners, limned
by colors fine and bright, limbed in lace and silk and cotton
to flower its curves and cleavage and comeliness.

I sing the fat self that thumps with a great triumphant splash
into creeks, rivers, lakes and oceans, spraying eddies
and currents and waves as the water sloshes over its luscious
wealth of skin and muscle and heft. I sing the self
that rends the air as it spills up to balance a serve, aims clear,
smacks, spikes and volleys and digs the ground,
its strong fat haunches planted sleek and fast as it
passes to players, then bounds up and anchors the net. I
sing the self that runs newly-dried turf, fit, fat and swinging
from base to base after batting over heads and hands and heaps
of scrambling fans.

I sing the fat self that sows, rends, reaps, harvests, mulling each
seed and petal and plant it worked into earth wetted and
mulched and mowed into wide waiting warmth. I sing the self
that once molded, still molds clay into loving fat women with
plentiful breasts and hips and thighs and
furred organs of pleasure.

I sing the fat self that wells into city streets, its arms akimbo
with briefcase and cellphone and printouts of stately, high,

thick buildings yet to be born. I sing the self that struts
high on scaffolds after welding metal and glass into
windows and rafters and beams and partitions, its muscled
arms and strong, succulent chest pointing to where the
next fire will take wood and make of it a tower.

I sing the fat self that feeds its lovely fat children and their
friends, that hugs its plump grandmother with her soft
cheeks and gently knowing hands. I sing the self that
argues for its right to stay fat and free, the self that celebrates
growth, nurturing, strength, fullness, roundness. I sing the
self that raises its voice for all who are spurned,
hated, disliked, ostracized, ignored.

I sing the fat soul.

FRANNIE ZELLMAN

"Did you lose weight?"
"Oh my god, did I lose it again?
Try the couch cushions…"

LESLEIGH J. OWEN

"Did you gain weight?"
"Why? Do you want to know my secret?"

KATHY BARRON

"Do you see a human being
when you look at me?
Or just a thing
to be changed,
carved,
molded
into some form
of cookie-cutter perfectionism?"

KATHY BARRON

I Am Mother Earth

I am Mother Earth.

Here is my body.
My breasts are rolling hillsides. Jiggle and shake with every
       quake.

My lightning thoughts pulse and crack and boom.

I am a big woman.

My hips as wide as the sheltering sky.
The vast expanse of the fierce Serengeti
casts its shadow across my belly.

Each and every bud and bloom comes from the life force
       of my womb.
There is majesty in the massive size of my mountainous thighs.

Herds of BBQ antelope—
forests of fruit til I burst.
Rivers of lava quench my thirst.

I am the very essence of Perfection.
Destruction.
Creation.
Elation.

Corinna Makris

"Did you lose weight?"
"No. Periodically my weight shifts itself
like plate tectonics."

LESLEIGH J. OWEN

"Did you gain weight?"
"Why? Are you looking for some?"

KATHY BARRON

ODE TO MY UPPER ARMS

Wings that fly me to another place
where amazons run naked and free,
laughing with lips stretched wide
like the merging of two great rivers
that rise and fall in ambiguous ripples,
stealthy movement over hard, parched soil,
while their servants sway in the hot sun,
sinuous snakes dancing to the flautist's song
their skin reddened, tender, and pliant,
dry and drowsy as a stranger's kiss—
or:
Baskets of rolls in which I tuck secret things:
Jealousies, memories of Shakespeare classes, forbidden swear
      words,
birthday gifts from years ago that still smell of my father,
opportunities to run for president,
to stamp my grinning visage on precious silver coins,
to nourish a continent,
to drink honeyed wine till my eyes blur
with dreams of equality—
or:
A magical plant from Venus,
spilling and fulfilling expectations,
eyes lowered, mouth pursed,
body crumpled like a wrecked car,
luring with promises of sameness...
before snapping my jaws closed,
cracking them together like an exclamation point
at the end of a long, long sentence—
or:
Salty loaves of sourdough bread
(that Jesus sure as hell didn't use

to feed the masses)
My taste—finite, precious, exclusive—
coats your tongue and leaves you
thirsting
Fragrant salt, crunching between your teeth,
dulling and loosening your tongue,
swimming through sinuses before nestling
in the hot sands of your brain—
Salt:
Invaluable spice,
smothering the twinkle of gold,
preserving, restoring,
desiccating
Turned into salt for daring to open my eyes,
needing to see for what
my daughters were sacrificed,
for crying humid tears
and spilling my prayers on the sand
with a tinkle that
destroyed the world—
or:
Soft and lumpy like pink-striped down pillows:
Warm, tangy, receptive, affirming,
comforting, blank, and supporting,
closing round your head
like ten Our Fathers
mumbled by rote—
or:
Mounds of bean-bag warmth,
that mirror my mother:
Gentle, generous flutterings
that brush the face like a butterfly's passing,

that soothe and cloy
like well-meant advice—
or:
Scratchy sighs
that whisper millennia's worth of untold stories:
Bedtime fairy tales
or songs of revolution?

LESLEIGH J. OWEN

"Did you lose weight?"
"Sadly, it fell down a well
and Lassie is trying to rescue it."

LESLEIGH J. OWEN

"Did you gain weight?"
"Why? Are you finding me more sensual
and luscious than ever?"

KATHY BARRON

PRIORITIES

I live
to love,
to make love,
and to eat—
the order
varies
by the moment.

KATHY BARRON

"Did you lose weight?"
"Heaven forbid!
There's not enough of me to go around as it is."

Lesleigh J. Owen

"Did you gain weight?"
"Why? Having a hard time controlling yourself
around my abundance?"

Kathy Barron

"Do you see a person
with hopes
and dreams
thoughts and feelings?
Or just your own ideas
of who I should be?"

Kathy Barron

My Vulgar Love

He once apologized
that his belly wasn't hard and flat.
Are you kidding me?!?

I love how substantial he is.
I love how his belly sticks out—
a barrel beckoning to me
to climb on and take a ride.
Desire in the form of man-flesh.
Makes me crazy with lust.

He once thought he would be more appealing
if he looked younger and thinner.
He knows better now.

I love the gray flecks in his hair,
the fullness of his face and body
as it ages and takes on the form
of a life well-lived and well-loved.
I love his thickness, his thighs, his ass.
I want him naked, next to me, all of the time.

I am queer enough
that his man-boobs thrill me.
I love it when we lie face to face,
our boobs squishing into each other,
making the most beautiful picture.
I love it when he hovers above me,
and I play with his breasts,
taking them into my mouth.
They aren't as soft as mine,
but still a delightful mouthful.

Ah, sweet sensuality
as I pull at his flesh with my teeth,
lick at his flesh with my tongue.
I love that he is not tight and taut—
that I can pull his flesh away from his body,
devouring him with my lust.
His body is my playground,
my sensual delight.
Love-making or simply lying naked,
spooning into each other,
taking turns in direction,
soft flesh melding into soft flesh,
total physical intimacy.

I can't get close enough to him,
need to feel him around me,
need to feel him inside me.
This is my vulgar love.
This is my pure love.

KATHY BARRON

Mirror, Mirror

An earthy, breathing image
of wonderland
like nothing Rubens ever painted.
I turn my head and see her:
Drowsy, sated, fat goddess
lying on her side,
breasts straining toward the soft tousle
of hotel bed covers,
reddened eyes spilling into mine,
laughing, her teeth inside her sore red lips
and above her chafed chin
as white as the
puckered expanse
of kneaded bread dough belly.
I reach toward her
and she toward me,
clasping each other's smooth, cool hands,
we whisper giggling, sisterly secrets
above the gentle hiss
of falling water.

Lesleigh J. Owen

Mirror, Mirror, part 2

Sorry to offend
Best I should crush my passions
Beneath metal veils

Just cuz I act like a girl
Don't mean I don't know how to kick your ass, sweetheart.
I got a thick layer of concrete
Stretching beneath this doughy white skin.
Better watch what you say,
Else I'll hammer you into a flat sheet of metal,
Only good for reflecting
The triumph of my foremothers
Stretching my mouth toward the sky.

Lesleigh J. Owen

"Did you lose weight?"
"I try to think of it as 'misplaced'
rather than "lost."

LESLEIGH J. OWEN

"Did you gain weight?"
"Do you think so? Let's have a party!"

KATHY BARRON

"Do you see me
for who I am?
Or do you just see
what you wish I were,
what you think I could be?"

KATHY BARRON

PART II
BIG FAT BITCH

NO ONE'S GAIA

mother goddess round as the earth
spinning like some bloodied top,
faster and faster,
melting away the world's miseries
in the fires of martyrdom

mother goddess sister lover
fat fecund body flowing forth,
filling the cracks
like a thumb in a leaky dike

sister mother wife victim
two halves clinging together
pinched at the bottom into the
pulsing shape of a heart

I   am   n o o n e ' s   e a r t h
m o t h e r

no one's good little girl,
Joan of Arc,
obedient house servant,
anthropological Venus
my fat strong childless body,
tall enough to eclipse the sun,
wide enough to crowd an entire world,
is not available for purchase,
not open for business,
not underdeveloped,
not ready for construction,

not wet, fresh soil
yearning for the farmer's plough

my arms, strong enough to snap a stake,
to smother a fire,
snap against my body like thunder,
shaking to dust those small-framed homes
built on sand and gossip

my tree trunk thighs
will never shelter the masses
can never split far enough, fast enough
to satisfy all the toothy, screaming mouths,
the sharp, metallic bodies
the wet, wagging tongues,
the voracious, vampiric appetites

I am no one's proxy mother,
no Oedipal drama waiting
to inspire a Greek chorus
no humans may enter
the earthy forest between my legs
where trees groan
and grasses sigh their desires
I offer no one a warm, comfortable teat
as pillow for the head,
pacifier for the mouth,
nourishment for the belly

my opened mouth gleams like a mirror
reflecting the heat
that radiates like fire

from my strong
fat body
my torso waxes and wanes,
a dusty moon
refusing to
enlighten the masses

Lesleigh J. Owen

"Did you lose weight?"
"Once the jiggling stops, you'll see
all is in order."

LESLEIGH J. OWEN

"Did you gain weight?"
"Wouldn't know.
I don't weigh myself."

KATHY BARRON

FAT BITCH

"Fat Bitch!"?
That's all you got?
I eat "fat bitch" like a cookie,
the crunchy sweetness satisfying all the way down—
with a nice sugar buzz when it hits my bloodstream.

Yeah, I'm a fat bitch, all right.
I won't get out of your way.
I won't change myself to make you feel better.
I won't take your shit.
And I most assuredly won't feel ashamed.

I'm a fat bitch
who holds her head high
and knows who I am
and is not intimidated by some
small-minded bully trying to intimidate
with hate and ignorance.

I'm a fat bitch
who eats what she likes
and makes love when she wants
and lives and loves OUT LOUD.
I'm a fat bitch who won't
shut up or get out of your way.

"Fat Bitch!"?
Why thank you!
I couldn't have said it better myself.
I'm not here to please you.
Your opinion of me is not my concern.

This fat bitch is here to live
MY life on MY terms.
Fat Bitch, indeed.

KATHY BARRON

"Did you lose weight?"
"Yes, but I'm hoping
someone will respond to my posters
and find it again…"

Lesleigh J. Owen

"Did you gain weight?"
"Why yes, I have!
I've gained about
eight or nine hundred pounds,
give or take a few hundred."

Kathy Barron

"Do you see
my strengths
my beauty
my passion?

Do you see
my struggles
my pain?"

KATHY BARRON

BIG FAT BITCH

I am not a nice or good fat woman.
I do not have a friendly bone in my body.
I do not cook. I hate playing with babies.
I am not eager to do kindnesses.
I do not pretend sweetness.
I do not give easily or happily of my time or ideas.
I like to shut the windows, bar the doors and grab a book.
I do not exercise. I do not eat healthy foods,
        whatever those are.
I do not have large soft breasts.
I don't have a fluffy yielding belly or round red cheeks.
I do not bring home baked bread to gatherings.
I don't do merry.
I walk fast and frown and make angry faces
        at people in my way.
I tend to order in and eat the rest of the pizza for breakfast—
        cold.
I elbow my way into subways and push thinner passengers
        aside.
I do not apologize in any way shape or form
        for what or who I am.
I am fat and likely to remain so, which poses absolutely
        no problem for me.
I am a bitch and likely to remain so, which also poses
        absolutely no problem for me.
Eat shit, world. And down the rest of your assumptions with it.
I leave no room for you.

FRANNIE ZELLMAN

"Did you lose weight?"
"Perish the thought!"

LESLEIGH J. OWEN

"Did you gain weight?"
"I gained some
then lost some and gained some more,
gained some, then lost some
and gained even more…
quite a few times."

FRANNIE ZELLMAN

"One day
the bigots, naysayers, soul-hungry
will find someone else to pick on.
To fill their diseased, shrunken minds
and their need to spread hatred,
people they can smear or belittle or degrade.

Or maybe, just maybe
by that time
they will not find anyone
at all."

FRANNIE ZELLMAN

Used to be a Nice Girl

I used to be a nice girl.
I'd blurt, "sorry!"
when someone bumped into me,
apologize for my existence,
smile automatically
all of the time,
even when others were rude—
like some zany poster for happy living—
smile, smile, smile.

"Nice girls care about
how **other** people feel."
"Nice girls don't think
about themselves,
their own feelings
or needs."
"Nice girls don't have desires…
except the desire to serve."
I tried very hard to be a nice girl.

Being nice
really wasn't the thing for me.
My hands were raw and sore,
bursting with eczema
from unexpressed rage—
at least, that's Louise Hay's best guess.
It fits.
My hands are healthy now—
rage does not go unexpressed.

Nice girls laugh quietly.
I laugh loudly

and even snort.
Nice girls sit politely
with their legs together.
I'm not a fan of gender based manners
and closing my legs
has never felt right to me.
I like taking up space
and being comfortable
even if it throws things
out of order.

Nice girls are thin
and pretty,
unassuming
and demure.
Not me, baby.
I'm fat and free,
wild, a little crazy
and not a demure bone in my body.
I assume much.

I was never cut out to be nice,
now that I think about it—
even though I tried very hard
to be
a nice girl.
The cost was too great.
And one day,
I just said screw it.
I'm not a nice girl anymore.
Not even close.

KATHY BARRON

FAT POETS SPEAK

"Did you lose weight?"
"Heck no! I'm not that irresponsible."

LESLEIGH J. OWEN

"Did you gain weight?"
"Why? Do I look more formidable,
more huggable, more cuddly?"

KATHY BARRON

PART III

IN A THIN-LOVING WORLD:
POEMS OF HURT & HEALING

No Reason to Feel

"You've got no reason
to feel sad,"
is what people said.
"You've got enough food, nice clothes,
parents who love you
and your own room with your very own bed."

"There are millions of kids in the world
who would love to trade places with you."
My tears couldn't escape, they stayed in my head.
I couldn't explain, couldn't express,
Couldn't feel anything anymore.
Just wished I were dead.

"You've got no reason
to be so happy.
You're just not that good."
In those moments
it became quite clear…
I knew I'd never feel completely loved or understood.

"You've got no reason
to feel like giving up.
You're lucky to live in your neighborhood!
You're spoiled and ungrateful.
That's what you are."
Explain? I would love to—if only I could!

"You've got no reason
to think you know anything.
You've seen some of the world, so what?
Your feelings and thoughts don't matter.

Your Truth to others is mindless chatter.
You're invalid, alone, a misguided nut."
 "You've got no reason
to feel angry."
May I bleed when I'm cut?
May I cry when I hurt?
May I live my own life?
May I break out of this rut?

"You've got no reason
to feel rage
or any other emotion so strong.
No reason to whine.
No reason to shout!"
Will I ever, ever, EVER feel like I belong?

I've got no reason
to feel anything.
I am always "wrong."
I can't express myself.
I can't do or feel anything "right."
I'm not allowed to sing my song.

Nobody knows me.
They never have.
They only ever looked at me from the outside.
Never got what it is to be me.
Never cared what I thought or felt.
My full humanity denied.

The only thing I ever wanted
was to be seen, to be heard

to be understood and recognized.
To be loved and accepted
for the fullness of who I am.
I can't even tell you how hard I tried.
I am strong. I am smart.
I have a soul, a pulse, a heart.
I've had experiences and pain
that have shaped who I am.
I see the world uniquely as I imagine you do too.
I too feel both the sunshine and the rain.

In fact,
I feel everything.
Even if you think I have no reason or no right.
I quite often feel too much.
Feel confused, feel frustrated
and sometimes feel like I'm spoiling for a fight.

My feelings are my own
as are my opinions, thoughts and beliefs
and I will not explain or apologize.
You can think what you want. Judge me how you will.
But you don't know me or my life.
You have NEVER seen anything through my eyes.

You can sit with me now
and we can share who we are.
Our understanding and friendship can rise
up out of prejudices and blindness,
out of apathy and fear,
out of the entrapment of lies.

We don't need a reason
to feel what we feel.
Our feelings are OURS.
Our lives are our own to create how we wish.
Being aware of and sharing our feelings
Is one of our greatest powers.

KATHY BARRON

To My Grandma Helen
(Helen Glaser, in memory, 1900–1988)

The waning hours approach,
when we used to play solitaire
and you used to let me play your cards
and we both laughed together
at nothing special
when neither of us could sleep.
You kept warning me to lose weight
and get my Ph.D.
I kept telling you that I would get it
in time
but kept silent about the weight
because I didn't know what to say to you,
my gently plump grandma
whose hugs enveloped me in love
from the day I was born.
Nanny, as I called you,
you did your own beautiful shape injustice
when you harped on losing weight
and worried about lies told by the scale.

But you went right on preparing those amazing dinners
until the day before you died
as if your own mind and body knew better.

More than eighteen years have gone by.
When it rains before dawn I think of you
and your wonderful softness heals me again
even if some of your words ran contrary
to the message your body gave.

In these wet foggy hours
Your fat granddaughter hugs you once more
in thought
and keeps missing you.

FRANNIE ZELLMAN

"Did you lose weight?"
"I'm too fabulous to whittle down."

Lesleigh J. Owen

"Did you gain weight?"
"Why? Do I look stronger, more powerful,
like I'm taking up more space
in the world?"

Kathy Barron

FREEZING IN THE SUN

January day, 1979.
The sun pours down on the icebound slate.
In the Bronx schoolyard,
We sit across from each other.
"Why are you smiling?" you ask.
"Because."
My breasts under my winter coat
heave in and out. I could die right now,
happy if we touched.

No matter how many girlfriends you have,
you never close yourself entirely.
Your eyes sweep me into wanting.

Reckless and determined,
I put out a hand.
But the hater inside stops me
cold
and whispers
that you don't like fat women
anymore.

2006.
The hater is dead.
We have not spoken in years.

I call your work number,
found on Google,
and let it ring.
Your message comes.

"Hi," I say, "remember me?"

I leave my words, but no info.

The lover in me touches you, finally,
after all this time,
as if summoning the winter sun,
then bows and retreats.

In phone space it is quiet and cold.

Frannie Zellman

"Did you lose weight?"
"Are you kidding? I ain't no loser!"

LESLEIGH J. OWEN

"Did you gain weight?"
"I've gained presence and power
and self-confidence and self-love."

KATHY BARRON

En Vogue

like a big elevator
everyone facing forward
it's just me clearing my throat
to show you I don't notice
I won't butt in
I don't know you
I don't care

clothes don't fit anymore
wrong size, wrong shape
belts to cinch your waist
girdles to hide your vices
shoes too tight
skirt too short
god, woman, what's that perfume you're wearing?

shiny faces in a dry ice fog
waiting for someone to yell "cut"
waiting for the theme music
you messed up your goddamn lines
again

made-up faces as flat as a shiny elevator door
or a TV screen
flicker away
seven second limit
clichés take five

skinny white blondes
like negatives of their shadows
is that a golden halo
or the reflection

of a camera bulb?

love means never having to say I'm sorry
radio songs don't mean anything
just chatty DJs
and contests I've never won
I won't butt in
I don't know you
I'm sorry

sealed in an envelope
clear black letters
smooth white face
gummy label
one sheet of paper folded in on itself
I know your destination, little girl

I used to cry golden tears
but I bottled them up
and sold them for a thousand dollars
an ounce

LESLEIGH J. OWEN

"Did you lose weight?"
"Nope, I gained smarts."

LESLEIGH J. OWEN

"Did you gain weight?"
"I might look bigger…
because my spirit is bigger
and my body is free."

KATHY BARRON

FAT BEAUTY

1: Oh my god, did you see her?

2: She had seven yards of bright pink crinkled rayon draped over her body, sweetie. How could I not see her?

1: I have one word of advice to give to Miss Pink Elephant: Jenny Craig.

2: I have one word of advice: Visit a gym once in a while.

1: That so wasn't one word.

2: Whatever.

1: Look at her cram herself into that booth! You think the management will have to call the fire department to get her out?

2: [snickering] Stop it! You're horrid!

1: Or maybe smear butter all over her and pop her out of the booth like a champagne cork?

2: Oh my god, that's hilarious. You know, I can't remember the last time I ate butter.

1: Ha! I bet you sure as hell can remember the last time you drank champagne.

2: I used to eat toast every morning when I was a kid, warm toast from the oven with butter spread all over it.

1: An oven?

2: It was a toaster oven. Anyway, on Sundays, my mom would make us cinnamon toast, which was really just warm toast with loads of butter, sugar, and cinnamon. I always ate the heel of the loaf, since I loved bread, and sometimes my brother would let me have his crusts.

1: Imagine the carbs! The fat grams!

2: No kidding. My thighs are spreading just reliving this.

1: Like your thighs spreading is unusual.

2: Ha! Look at her now. She's just sitting there, all huge and pink and crammed in a booth. Oh sure, go ahead, get your book from your bag. Have a nice read, a gargantuan lunch. Don't worry about drawing attention to your massive self by cheerfully waddling through a restaurant wearing neon pink.

1: What do you want to bet she orders the appetizer platter and eats it all herself?

2: Or a burger and fries?

1: Disgusting! All that oily, fatty, breaded, rich stuff. She's absolutely shameless, sitting there all calm, smiling like an idiot while she reads her stupid book, the tabletop squeezed between her rolls. Thank god she's wearing Pepto pink; maybe it'll help stifle my nausea.

2: I wonder if she's ever seen lettuce outside of a burger.

Maybe you should offer her the rest of your salad, since
you only ate half.

1: The waitress put too much salad dressing on it. I told her
no more than a teaspoon.

2: You want the rest of my fruit cup? It was okay, but the
pineapple could have been a little fresher.

1: No, I'm totally full, thanks. Oh my god, look at Pinky,
joking with the waitress. What do you think they're
saying?

2: She's probably asking the waitress if the cook knows how
to deep-fry a chicken.

1: Look at the book she's reading—something about beauty.
Girlfren, give it up; beauty's in another zip code right
now.

2: "Hello, is this beauty? You've reached a number that
has been disconnected. Please hang up and try your call
again."

1: No kidding! If she's looking for beauty tips, I could
have saved her some time and money. It's pretty simple,
pumpkin: lose the pink, lose the weight, lose the goofy
smile, lose the book.

2: Or else grow out your hair! Someone that size needs a
curtain to hide behind, a pillowcase for your pillowy face.

1: You are so catty! I was just going to say hit the gym,

munch on a few salads, let nature take its course.

2: And wear some respectable black. Someone that size does not need to be drawing attention to herself. My mother always used to tell me that vertical stripes and black are both slimming.

1: What about black vertical stripes? Does that turn you into a supermodel?

2: Ha-ha. Notice how I always wear black, and it always makes me look good, right? Right?

1: I think her book says something about how beauty is a myth.

2: At least she's being honest with herself.

1: How can beauty be a myth? I mean, didn't what's-her-name's face launch a thousand ships in Greece or Rome or wherever?

2: Not literally, I hope. That would hurt like hell.

1: Do you want me to throw my unsweetened iced tea on your slimming black top? I'm talking about beauty, as in Audrey Hepburn, the Taj Mahal, or Tyra Banks or something. It can't be a myth. That doesn't make sense. If beauty were a myth, how would we know the Australian Opera House is beautiful? Why would everyone want to go see the Grand Canyon or surf online for paintings by famous artists like Picasso, Da Vinci, and that one guy—Rubens?

2: Honey, beauty is a myth—for some women. For the rest of us, it's an uphill battle we fight every day. After all, some of us have to march in the army of beauty. I'm a beauty warrior. Pink elephant over there, she's a beauty casualty. Collateral damage.

1: And everyone knows supermodels are beautiful, right? I mean, if beauty is a myth, how come everyone agrees that Heidi Klum is gorgeous? My god, she's almost six feet tall, weighs no more than 125, and has long brown hair. How could this not be beautiful?

2: You're overthinking this, sweetie. Of course beauty isn't a myth. I mean, come on! If beauty weren't real, then what would be the point of padded bras? Pantyhose? Black wardrobes that cast all little tucks and pooches into shadow?

1: No kidding! If beauty was some great myth, then everyone would be eating cheeseburgers at lunch and wearing retina-scarring colors!

[pause]

2: Thank god that book title is full of it.

1: Thank god.

[pause]

1: Do you mind if I have just one or two bites of your fruit cup?

LESLEIGH J. OWEN

"Did you lose weight?"
"Yes, several times before realizing
how ridiculous it is."

LESLEIGH OWEN

"Did you gain weight?"
"All the weight from not dieting
went to my brain.
Try it some time!"

FRANNIE ZELLMAN

"If fatness causes heart disease,
then all fat people
would be clutching our chests
and dropping over dead.
And thin people would never die
of a heart attack."

KATHY BARRON

"One day
they will tell us
that dieting was a myth
and that happy, healthy people
of all sizes
eat what they want when they want
and really don't think or worry it
like some squirrel in winter gnawing an acorn."

FRANNIE ZELLMAN

HALF

Pardon me
I don't mean to bother you
but I've lost someone.
I don't know where she's gone.
Maybe you've seen her?
You can't miss her:
Curly brown hair,
a gap between her front teeth—
well, you probably didn't notice,
if you didn't have a conversation,
but she does tend to laugh
a lot.
She's about 5'7", give or take,
though some say she looks a little taller.
And, well, I probably shouldn't say—
I mean, it's what's on the inside, right?—
but she's kinda, well, you know,
chubby,
plump,
kind of, you know,
overweight…
not that it makes her any less of a person
or anything;
I just thought you might have seen her.

Are you sure?
I really think she might have come this way.
Please try to remember.
She would have been wearing orange,
or maybe hot pink,
and carrying a lime green purse.
Just describing her, I can just picture her

fluttering like a tropical parrot,
or a bird of paradise—
the bird, I mean, not the flower.
The flower is pretty and all,
but she's definitely more like a bird,
especially because she sings
a bunch
and loudly,
like no one is listening
or maybe like everyone is
and she's some kind of girl band unto herself
or maybe Sarah Brightman—
I'm sorry?
Two Sarah Brightmans? Ha—that's funny.

No, I don't have a picture on me
but she's quite easy to remember.
She has brown eyes,
at least, that's what her driver's license says;
well, it says "bro,"
but you know what I mean.
Truthfully, they're light brown
with smears of green,
but she doesn't like green eyes
and forbids anyone to mention it.
She says green is the rarest eye color
and brown the most common;
she says she would rather take
something everyone has
and celebrate the beauty
of its commonness.
Personally, I've always been partial to blue.

I'm certain you would know her
if you could hear her laugh.
She starts out with a giggle
and then gains momentum
until a laugh spins out of her
like fireworks
across a dark sky.
She clutches her stomach and rocks,
hee heeing while laughter
shoots out of her mouth
like pellets from a shotgun—
you know: "Ha. Ha. Ha. Ha. Ha."

She should be easy to remember,
a big girl and all
with glaring clothes,
brown eyes,
(brownish green, but don't tell her I said so)
and a booming voice.
I don't know what I'll do
if I can't track her down.
I've known her all my life,
watched her buy her flashy clothes
from the fat girl outlet stores—
terribly awkward for me,
as I'm sure you can imagine—
listened to her sing in the shower
as if auditioning for a duet
with none less than Pavarotti,
shrank with shame when she chose
bright purple flip-flops
over delicate high heels,

murmured apologies
when she peppered people
with her raucous laughter.

What? Oh, she sounds it, doesn't she?
Sure, she's embarrassing and all,
with her loudness, her laughter,
the way she wears bright yellow
like there's nothing wrong with
weighing 300 pounds,
or how being with her
makes it so much harder
to rely on clichés
and sink into backgrounds.
Plus, there's the way she seems to
carry her own spotlight
with her,
celebrating the beauty
of her commonness.
Yes, I've been mortified
on countless occasions…
but nothing has been the same
since she left.

Well, I'm sorry to have bothered you.
I guess you haven't run into her.
You surely would have remembered her;
it seems no one can forget.
In fact, just yesterday a young man
I barely knew
came up to me and asked me
to sing one of her songs.

I tried—I even remembered the lyrics!—
but I couldn't muster the air
to whirl the notes to his ears.
Geez, it's really too bad
you never got to meet her;
she's a riot and a half.
Everyone who knows her misses her,
asks about her.
And me, well,
all I know is
I feel like half a person
since she left.

LESLEIGH J. OWEN

Did You Lose Weight? (1)

No, did you find any?
Is weight for sale this month?
I think they tend to have excellent weight downtown,
close to the Lower East Side, where they used to sell
it from pushcarts, near the hot chestnuts and cold pickles.
They sold weight then for two cents, but it soon inflated
    with demand.

Now I buy my weight in a particular place in the Bronx
when I manage to get up there. One takes the 6 train,
    then a bus.

If you find some good weight on sale, please do tell me.
I simply can't tell
what it looks like from the catalogues.

DID YOU LOSE WEIGHT? (2)

Yes, I lost weight.

Now I weigh about as much as some
of the concentration camp survivors
who made it to the USA on the quota
in 1945. The rest had to stay in Europe.
Or if they were lucky, they made it to Israel,
then called Palestine,
on leaky boats
and weren't sent to Cyprus
to stand behind barbed wire and remember.

Now I weigh as much
as I weighed at nine
when I was heavier and taller
than two of the counselors
at camp. Only then I was strong enough
to run around and catch well
and hate rest hour.

Now I weigh as much
as a quarter of a cow hung in a stall
in Karachi. You point,
and they cut the part you want.
My arms, however, are too thin
to yield stock for soup.

Now I weigh as much
as two street dogs
who nose in garbage
by day
and sleep in alleys

by night, dreaming
of raw meat and spoiled milk.
Now I weigh about as much
as a brace of hummingbirds
who are so light
that they can stop in midair
then fly backwards.

But when I tried to turn,
I only ended up spraining
my ankle
because my bones became too brittle
to flex.

FAT POETS SPEAK

DID YOU LOSE WEIGHT? (3)

Shout

I saw them
my sisters,
counting calories and glycemic values
and vitamin equivalents
as if they were numbers
that would lead them magically
to healthy lives
but even more so
to the magic weight
at which they would no longer be screamed at
or laughed at
or spat on.

I saw them
my sisters
counting seconds minutes hours days
starving time by starving themselves
in the hope that time would pass somehow
without food
and without wanting.

I saw them
my sisters
having their stomachs stapled
and their jaws wired shut
in the hopes
that they wouldn't be hungry
or tempted
to take a bite of toast
or a slice or fruit,

as if they could live on dreams
and air.
I saw them
my sisters
shuttling back and forth
between doctors and hospitals
as their insides crumbled
and staples slid open
and the doctors admonished them
for not sticking to the program.

I saw them
my sisters
running up hills and down hills
treadmilling five times a day
pummeling their stomachs
squeezing their calves
as they tried to exercise themselves
into some woman-hater's ideal
of what their bodies
should resemble.

I saw them
my sisters
scorned at designer shops
as salespeople
with sneering voices
and pursed lips
and shrivelled hands
chained to thinness
told them
that the latest fashions

didn't come in their size.

I saw them
my sisters
trying to join
movements for change,
working sixty hours a week
to bring food and shelter to others
only to be ignored, ridiculed
and shunted aside
because their size was "their fault."

Then I saw them
my sisters
mouthing those first words,
"Why do they hate us?
Is fat so bad?
Why are they trying
to change us?"
What do they want
of us?"

And I saw them
my sisters
pronouncing those next words,
"Why do we hate ourselves?
What can we do to change our lives?"

and then:
"What do we want for ourselves?"
"What can we do to change
our world?"

I saw them
my sisters
I saw them
and then finally
finally
I heard them.

Frannie Zellman

"Did you lose weight?"
"I used to, but I got over it."

LESLEIGH OWEN

"Did you gain weight?"
"Let me see how much water
I displace when I go swimming
and I'll tell you."

FRANNIE ZELLMAN

PART IV

IN A MELLOW MOOD:
FAT & WONDERFUL SEASON

CERES

Autumn's smooth, puffy bronze cheeks,
salty sweet chin
Gently creaking sounds of awakening,
Bones groaning like the cracking
of a rusty cellar door,
Autumn, with her dusty-wheat-scented breaths,
whose round, curving, gently drooping body
polishes the world into
smooth, gray contours.
Her eyes,
like newly-discovered amber
with never-popped air bubbles,
warm the room like vanilla-scented candlelight
as she envelops the world in her
spicy rolls of flesh.
Summer's not the time for me:
Sunlight that casts angular shadows in wide-open mouths
No more feeling the scrape of sand
sloughing over my dense curves,
trying to whittle down my folds of flesh
into smooth, plastic expanses of cookie cutter skin.
No more poppy-scented laughs
that chime like dissonant dinner bells
and abrade my delicate ears.
Bright white light
take away my sight.
Thin, hungry, sweaty bodies,
arms shaking, smiles flaking, biceps quaking,
frozen in flashes of sunlight on teeth.
False idols of perfection
that die before they can ever
live a full-bodied life.

Autumn, that sweet, round, wise, dangerous old woman
arrives slyly in her orange, Cinderella-like pumpkin—
as round and majestic as people—
tossing dried, crackling, russet leaves like confetti or candy:
Throw me something, grandmother!

Autumn: Happy, crisp, nutmeg, rounded season.
My mouth opens and closes in happy little Os
over words like "orange" and "clove,"
circular, bouncing words,
round, rich, and warm.
Leaves bend and snap beneath my ponderous weight
while the scent of earth weaves like cinnamon
through my sinuses.
Yawning, indolent light puffs gently through
twisted branches and desiccated leaves,
shining golden orange
like heaps of buttered, cinnamon-scented, steaming mashed
yams
or lightly-oiled strings of spaghetti squash.
Walking this cooling, linear stretch of sidewalk,
I am tempted to bite into the toothy, yellow winds
that crease around my body like well-starched sheets,
to jump high and far,
passing through the low-hanging laundry
snapping in the sky,
jump miles away from all scents of limestone and exhaust,
to throw my gray, woolen poncho over the clouds
and roll in the decaying scent of leaves
that stick to my face
like allspice on a baker's hands.
I can finally breathe beneath this nubby grayness

that stretches like a fluffy headscarf
over the dome of the sky.
Seasonal bounty,
Harvest time, time for rest.
Shelving our immature dreams
and discovering reverence for plenty
at night, I eat ginger carrot soup for supper
and slurp pumpkin custard from heirloom dishes.
My squash-shaped body—
honored for its softness,
its abundance,
its life-affirming heaviness—
snuggles into the scratchy red blanket
crocheted for me by my mother
while I bounce children and tradition
on my plump, arthritic knees
and sip cocoa and warm candlelight.
Fatness and autumn:
round, pumpkiny, bountiful:
a sensual feast.
Fatness and autumn—
lush and earth-scented as mounds of warm flesh—
dance together in gentle spirals
like leaves in a windstorm.
Come evening time, Autumn and I sit
like old friends,
cackling on the front porch,
bellies bouncing together
while heavy, purple mugs of chamomile tea
warm our loving, generous,
fleshy hands.

Lesleigh J. Owen

Yummy Fat Love

I eat Häagen-Dazs every day
to be absolutely sure
my rolls don't go away.

Not that they ever actually would.
They never have—no matter
how long I've been "good."

I delight in my every pound and curve.
My flesh, my fat, my lushness,
my desires, my appetites all I serve.

I am delicious and delightfully yummy
from my fat thighs to my luscious ass
to my pendulous breasts and rolls of tummy.

I am a sensuous feast to my hubba-lover
who teases, touches, bites, licks, sucks
and pleases me on **top** of the cover.

Lights on, fully exposed to the intimate gaze.
Beautiful flesh displayed boldly and barely…
desires rising to a sizzling blaze.

My fat body is a joy that I treasure.
It is my vessel of love, of sensual delight,
of intimacy and of infinite pleasure.

Kathy Barron

"Did you lose weight?"
"And make less of me to love?"

LESLEIGH OWEN

"Did you gain weight?"
"Oh, is that why you can't
push me
off the seesaw?"

FRANNIE ZELLMAN

FEAST OF FRUIT

Long watermelon thighs,
round, firm, heavy,
solid, ripe, weighty
roll apart easily
exposing
the tender fig
husband-lover pulls open
licking the fruit
before he sucks it
gently into his mouth,
pulling the fruit
away from the skin
steadily,
his tongue gripping
delicately.
Drinking.
Feasting.

Pear breasts
with peach nipples,
raspberry points,
sway gently
as the pumpkin belly
quivers.
Fat, round McIntosh arms
move freely
as though floating
in water
waiting to be claimed
with splashing teeth
and happy laughter.
Plum cheeks
and cherry lips

redden with desire
satiating.

KATHY BARRON

"Did you lose weight?"
"Yes, but I'm desperately awaiting the return
of my prodigal pounds."

LESLEIGH J. OWEN

"One day
they will tell us
what they know already,
but are too frightened—like rats
scurrying around subways,
with trains running on all tracks—
to say in public: that fat people live as long
or longer than slimmer people."

FRANNIE ZELLMAN

PART V

RECLAIMING & CELEBRATING OUR FAT SELVES

RAPUNZEL Revisited

Rapunzel, Rapunzel,
    do NOT let down your hair.
        Search not out your window;
            your rescue is not there.

Gaze instead in looking glass,
    your own eyes and heart to see.
        Say to her, there:
            Hello,
            I am,
            I am me,
            I be.
Claim your spirit; own your soul!
    In your magnificence, belief.
        Only in your own power
            will be found your relief.

Happiness' door is always open.
    Wait no more—you ARE the key.
        Go!—Greet the world:
        Hello!
            I am!
                I am ME!
                I BE!

Anne S. Kaplan

"Did you lose weight?"
"Gee, I don't know.
Did you have a bowel movement today?"

FRANNIE ZELLMAN

SHAME LIVED HERE ONCE

Shame lived here once
right here in this body,
right smack in the middle of my life.
Shame visited from time to time when I was little…
and moved in for good when I was twelve.
I remember the day that shame settled in
with all of its baggage and energy
and decided to stay.

Shame made itself right at home,
filling up little legs
and shining eyes,
wandering into every little thought,
into every tiny cell,
into every fiber of my being.

Shame whispered most of the time,
quietly poisoning my spirit,
yelled sometimes
demanding my full attention,
deafening my young ears
to the cries of my Soul.

Shame made it hard
to breathe
to think
to live.
Shame made my eyes
see only criticism
and pain.
Shame made me feel
self-hatred

and fear.

Shame made me look
at myself
and exclaim, "disgusting!"
Can you **imagine**?
A **human being** reduced to that level
of worthlessness?
Day in, day out,
over and over again.

Shame warred with my spirit,
fought with my sanity,
battled with me for years.
It was long and brutal.
Shame held nothing back,
nothing sacred.
Just attacked viciously.
Repeatedly.
And eventually, shame lost.
Burned itself out.
Left nothing more to take.

Shame doesn't live here anymore.
Doesn't even dare visit.
Shame is not welcome.
Shame does not exist
because shame has no power
over me
anymore.

Shame doesn't get to see

me in the tub,
my fat belly sticking well out of the water
which doesn't cover me,
my round thighs floating,
my strong, thick calves
big as the thighs of many men.

Shame doesn't get to look
at the new scar by my ribs
there near the center
just below my right breast.
Or at my breasts flopping across
my wide expanse of white abdomen,
the hair curling from my belly button down.

There are so many things
that shame would have died
to have pointed out.
What a laugh shame would have had
if it could have seen me
shaving my chin—
cause tweezing just doesn't cut it anymore.
Oh, the nothingness to which shame
would have reduced me.
But shame doesn't get to see that or to laugh.

What a frenzy shame would have had
if it could have made me cry and cringe
at my gray hair
or widening ass
or the betrayals of family and friends.
Shame would have rejoiced
as I gave up,

rolled over and died
the death of worthlessness.

But shame doesn't live here anymore.
And I'm not dying.
I'm not even sad or apologetic.
So I have hair growing
in places where I'd rather it didn't,
like on my face—
the same as about half the population on earth.
And I am fat,
which it turns out I rather like.
And I've had people in my life
who've misunderstood, misjudged, and mistreated me.
So what?

There is still no room for shame.
There is no reason for shame.
I'm not "perfect,"
whatever that means.
Wouldn't want to be even if it were possible.
I don't have all of the answers,
or maybe even any of them.
But I don't care about that either.
Shame still can't find me.

What I do know is this:
love and joy live here now.
Love surrounds me and permeates me
like shame used to do,
but love heals me
and encourages me
and cheers me on.

Joy makes me appreciate
every beautiful day,
and every aspect of myself.
Together, love and joy
let me look at myself and my life
and feel happy.

Shame lived here once,
but love and joy live here now
with me
forever.
I am beautiful.
I am human.
I am alive.
I am worthy.
Shame is just a distant memory.
Shame doesn't live here anymore.

KATHY BARRON

Making Movies

The woman's large soft dangling breast
rests in his strong muscled meaty hand.

The man's luscious flowing belly
touches her dimpled succulent thighs.

The woman's gently rippling bottom
kneads her husband's sleek wide chest.

Their creamy bodies shake and dissolve
into each other, the pooling massive, engorged,
wildly long.

One day their epitaph will read:
These two fat gorgeous people loved each other.
If you loved them, love yourself.

One day my epitaph will read:
This person loved fat people and found them gorgeous.
If you loved her, love them.

Frannie Zellman

No Magic Pill for Me

I do not want a magic pill, thanks anyway.
I want a magic wand!

I don't want to change my body, you see.
I want to change society!

I like my curves, my lush, soft flesh.
I like holding loved ones to my breasts.

I like my comfortable, heavy, strong reality.
There's not a thing I would want to change about me.

Ah. But a magic wand.
Now, with that I could change the world!

A flick of the wand and there would be
seats in ALL sizes and varieties.

Another flick of the wand would render
all aches, pains and diseases gone—blissful splendor!

A final flick of the wand and small, hateful thinking
would shift to a world that loves everyone, our hearts and
      souls linking.

Kathy Barron

I CELEBRATE
MY EVERY CURVE

This happened to me the other night.
A guy in a bar wanted to fight.
He gave me a look as if to say
that seeing me had ruined his day.
That he would rather kiss a toad
or lick the asphalt off the road
than sit at the bar knee to knee
with a girl as fat as me.

He said that I would look so pretty
if only I were itty bitty
and did I not realize the fact
that even though I am truly stacked
no man would ever really want me
because fat girls just aren't as sexy
as those other women with no hips
whose flat bellies make him lick his lips.

I suppose I could have made a scene,
maybe kick his leg and say things mean.
But then I thought that instead of spite
I'd consider his personal plight.
A man might feel betrayed or hurt,
shocked by his own desire to flirt
with a buxom curvy beauty
instead of a slender narrow cutie.

Bombarded on a daily basis
with images of smooth young faces,
certain the only shape he'd feel
has rock hard abs and buns of steel,

although he might long for a bride
with cleavage deep and backside wide,
coping with ridicule and abuse
a single man might get the blues.
Every magazine he's read
tells him to get me into bed
by finding some sort of common ground,
and surely no woman wants to be round.
So he thought he'd strike up a chat
about how terrible it is to be fat.
And while his pickup line was lame,
I refused to walk the path of shame.

I've got no interest in diet fads.
I change the channel on workout ads.
I'd rather have delicious lunches
than execute one hundred crunches;
Country walks and chats by the fire,
glasses of wine with friends who inspire.
I'll never agree to do without.
Being hungry makes me pout.

I told him that he would be surprised
by the softness of my thighs,
and yes I jiggle when I wiggle.
My body shakes with every giggle
and when I sit around the house
I know you're looking down my blouse.
So even though you've got some nerve,
I celebrate my every curve.

CORINNA MAKRIS

Venus Envy

I ain't your baby.
I can birth a baby
using nothing but the mastery
of my own body.
I can suspend that baby
above the cold and the pain
using only my arms.
I can nourish that baby
with the milk
that flows from my breasts.
I ain't your girl.
I can warm a girl
with the radiance
eddying within my curves.
I can comfort that girl
within the padded, muscled ring of arms
grown strong from holding her.
I can comfort that girl
by pressing her head to the plump breast
where sweet milk once flowed.
I can teach that girl
to use her mastery and her warmth
to be a smart, round, powerful woman
like me.

Lesleigh J. Owen

"One day
the words 'fat,' 'thin,' 'average,' 'slim,'
'heavy,' 'obese,' 'overweight,' 'underweight'
will be as archaic as counting head bumps
and one will use Oxford's
to locate their origins."

FRANNIE ZELLMAN

TURNING POINT

Labor Day, 1998, 4 AM.
Windstorm outside;
Ill-winds blow in here, too.

You, dear friend (for not much longer),
decline our business venture
because I won't play by your rules...

and You, supposed best friend for life,
instead critic and cynic of my work,
my mothering, my body, my being...

Rejected, betrayed, awash in self-pity,
bereft of value, overflowing with pain,
naught but bleak on the horizon...

Sleep—the only answer—endless, still.
This fistful of pills will stop my heart
and I will at last have peace.

I sit. Pill bottle empty, water glass full
death still in my hand...
should I leave a note or just go?

I sit. The tears stop. It is quiet.
The tiny voice says, not asks,
"wait four hours."

I sit. I wait. I sleep. I do not dream.
Pills back in bottle, and
the winds still blow.

Sun rises on a weird-orange sky;
branches and debris are everywhere.
Winds still blow; I wake.

And I know—death was here.
She who slept is no more,
replaced by someone else, someone new.

Death, birth, transformation.
Wind-fury births rage-fury
at loss that was and that was not.

Rage-fury says "Nevermore!"
My power is mine, alone;
no one else deserves it.

What others say, though hurtful,
will ne'er more rule my being
nor override what I know in here.

A week follows, a week of Spirit,
of trance, of guidance,
new view, new slogan, new life.

Labor Day, 2006, all day.
Now, at last, I know that voice—
she was the divine in me.

ANNE S. KAPLAN

Arctic New Year

When I was ten, I asked my sister
if clouds were the collected breaths of
every being in wintertime.
She laughed as she said no
and I watched her breath
flutter into the sky
like a hungry white raven.

My plumpness,
my comfort,
my warmth.
In cold winds, snowbound mornings, frozen Januaries—
days in which the sun hung motionless
like an air bubble in amber—
my insulation,
my fatness
used to shame me.

I remember huddling in the schoolyard,
gloveless, hatless,
cringing while tiny white talons
stabbed my flesh like icicles,
giggling children doing with fingers
what adults would later
do with words.

I learned to button my coat tight
and wreathe my stout neck—
where folds of flesh huddled together in solidarity—
with yards of scratchy fabric
and cram my large, strong, grasping hands
into anonymous white mittens.

I have traveled 3000 miles and two dozen years
to the frozen tundra
and the gray and white, argyle skies.

I wait for calmness and tranquility,
some kind of arctic Zen moment
in which I seek comfort and healing from
the spirit of my fat animal sisters:
the arctic seal, maybe, or perhaps the humpback whale.
Our spirits will hoot, hump, and sing
about cold-hearted, human predators,
about suckling our young,
about cross-species collaborations,
about finding relief and release
amongst the silvery mounds of snow
that rise and fall against the landscape
like warm, mammalian breasts.

Instead, I am exhilarated, breathless.
Lit with starlight and smoked breaths,
the sunless afternoon gleams expectantly
like a sweaty, hushed scene change
between musical numbers.

I plunge through the snow in my sandals.
Although I bought them in my size and width,
my expensive arctic boots huddle in the corner,
too small and narrow for my ample feet.

The snow groans and creaks
beneath my steaming feet.
The zipper on my coat has burst;

its puller lies small and impotent against my roaring bulk.
My belly arches between my coat halves
like a shout shattering a thought bubble.
A purple and red hat
flames atop my head
My chin perches merrily
above snuggling rolls of neck skin.

From my grinning, gap-toothed, gaping mouth
breaths writhe their smoky trails
about my head
while icicles snap beneath my feet.

This is no pantheistic or transcendent moment for me:
No communion with walruses,
waltzes with northern lights,
or metaphors of native blanket tosses.
For once, I am content to be me,
the eight-year old who buried her face in her hood,
the thirty-two year-old whose feet melt the snow,
the strong, laughing fat woman from L.A.
with the busted zipper,
perpetually overheated interior,
and undersized snow boots.

LESLEIGH J. OWEN

THE POETS—
ALPHABETICALLY

KATHY BARRON

I am at a place of enormous contentment in my life right now. I'm married to a wonderful man who is truly my soul mate. I have a darling teenage daughter with whom I am very close. The three of us have a lot of fun and laughs together.

I do have some challenges, as we live with and take care of my disabled mother. She is a lovely person, but having our lives tied down like this can be frustrating—and unless someone has been there, they can't possibly know what it's like. There are a few people (specifically my siblings) who are quick to criticize and to judge— and that can be very exasperating. Still, for the most part, life is happy and good.

I was an average sized teenager who always thought I was too fat. It didn't help that I was addicted to women's magazines (*Cosmo, Self, Seventeen,* etc.) or that I had a mother who was constantly trying to lose weight, or that my younger sister was naturally very thin. Much emphasis was placed in our family on the importance of being thin.

I started dieting around age 12, which is when I first felt any anxiety about the size or shape of my body. I dieted my way through my teens and twenties. I'd always been an athlete, so I played sports and exercised consistently. Still, my weight swung wildly, and I felt desperately miserable and hopeful about my body for close to two decades. My life was overshadowed in every way by my concern and despair about my weight.

Right after my daughter was born, when I was almost 30, I was first exposed to the concept of size acceptance. I read *When Women Stop Hating Their Bodies* and *Making Peace With Food.* Then I found NAAFA and *Radiance* magazine. I started to become very outspoken on the subject of size acceptance. I completely stopped dieting. I put up signs in my health food store about loving one's body at any size. I hit the highest weight of my life. Shortly thereafter, I found *Fat!So?* and Marilyn Wann. In 1997, I attended my first NAAFA convention. I was thrilled. That same year, I divorced and moved back home.

Back in my old hometown, with the attitudes of my family and community weighing on me, I lost my mind and lost 90 pounds. When I got very near my "goal" weight, I realized that I was *not* happy. I was not happy fighting with my body—it took all of my time and energy to be thin. And it wasn't even remotely worth it.

I dove eagerly back into size acceptance, reading books and having many conversations in an online fat-positive community. Over the years, size acceptance waxed and waned for me. I embraced it and then abandoned it. I struggled so much with my self-image and my body-image. And then, something just snapped, and that was it. I could no longer accept nor embrace any negativity about my body or about fatness. It all seemed so ridiculous to me. It just didn't make sense.

"Size acceptance" shifted into "fat acceptance" and "body liberation"—not just for me, but for many of the people I know. Ending fat oppression and the discrimination against fat people became very important to me. I could no longer see "weight loss" as anything harmless or benign. I started seeing the prejudice against fat people as "thin supremacy"—a civil rights issue, an ethical issue, a humanitarian issue. I now can't see it any other way.

It's been several years now since I've dieted. I have become very comfortable in my body, very happy with the word "fat," and proud to be a strong, fat woman.

My husband and I attended the NAAFA convention in 2006, where I met my wonderful group of fellow fat poets. I hadn't written much poetry in my life up until that summer. I mostly write my thoughts in essay form. But I've been having a lot of fun writing poems. In poems, you can say things that are nearly impossible to say any other way. It is a whole new world of communication—and I love it!

I look forward to a long and loving connection with this precious group known as the Fat Poets' Society.

Anne S. Kaplan

Known around the Internet as "Coach Anne," I am a Certified Personal Business and Life coach (CPCC). A "recovering scientist" (Ph.D. in neuroscience) and former computer programmer and consultant, I am now living my life purpose by empowering others; and I am doing so, finally, as an openly fat and proud woman.

As owner of ASK & Answer Coaching & Consulting, I will partner with anyone with the commitment, drive, and passion to change her/his life for the better.

In particular, I serve owners of microbusinesses, and, through the newest arm of my business—AmpleAliveness.com—women ready to reclaim their power from the word "fat."My blog and website are at http://amplealiveness.com—AmpleAliveness™ is an evolving invitation to join me on the journey from self-loathing to self-respect, -appreciation, and -celebration; from life deferred to some mythical day to life lived full out in the present.

Besides size acceptance/body diversity and Health at Every Size (HAES), some of my other interests include healthy cooking, spirituality, Sudoku, logic puzzles, purposeful living, community-building, public speaking, abundance, healing, wellness, self-care, body wisdom, wordplay, energy coaching approaches such as Emotional Freedom Techniques (EFT), ethical science and compassionate medicine, and heart-based living. My husband of 30 years and I, currently empty-nesters and owned by a beagle, are hoping to one day become grandparents.

People who know me now find me to be enormously caring, passionate, funny, serious, short, fat, earthy, intuitive, spiritual, an ADDult, and, every once in a while, wise; and I defy anyone—including myself—to say that "fat" is the most important word in that list. But it used to be, and I used to be a very different person.

For much of my life, "fat" was the only way I thought of myself, along with all I was taught "fat" meant—ugly, unlovable, unworthy. If you're reading this, you know what I mean. I was lonely and sad and angry and lost.

My shift towards a more accepting sense of self began with books like *Fat is a Feminist Issue, Overcoming Overeating,* and Geneen Roth's series. However, my most significant turning point (described in a poem by that name in this volume) came not very long ago, and only after hitting bottom.

The poem starts off very sad (as did I), but the sadness is not the point—rather, it's how despair, and survival, and the rage that was born from it, and the divine undercurrent to all of that, helped make me who I am today. Without having touched that darkness, I'd not have had that quantum shift and spiritual awakening.

One of the things born in the aftermath was my ferocious dedication to my own self- and size-acceptance, and the calling to serve people (instead of statistics and bits'n'bytes) and, eventually, people of size. The slogan mentioned in the poem—given to me that week in a dream—is the same one I still use to sign my emails:

"Become all you are, today; don't wait to be less."

CORINNA MAKRIS

Until my mid-20s I was a bit like Eeyore in Winnie the Pooh. Always expecting the worst and never disappointed when the worst inevitably arrived.

I tried to convince myself that I didn't care about having fun because I was supposed to work hard now and reap the rewards later, but truthfully, I was fun-deprived and I knew it. The lack of fun and the abundance of dissatisfaction in my life affected my emotional as well as my physical health.

Over the years I tried many different ways to improve my own self-esteem, and to have more fun. I walked the "get-well" path for many years

hoping to find a method that would fix what was wrong with me and help me feel good about myself. While I was grateful for the strides I made towards liking myself more, ultimately, I was not gratified. No matter how hard I tried to improve myself, fix what was wrong with me, or attempt to re-program myself with new behaviors and habits, the underlying theme remained the same. In order to "get well" I first had to admit that I carried something within me that I had to get rid of before I could be "okay." And then, maybe, if I was lucky enough to find a way to control whatever "fault" I had, then maybe I would have a chance of enjoying my life. It's depressing just talking about it, and living that way was even more difficult.

Throughout this period of my life I believed that losing weight was the only way that I would like myself more, and so I tried every diet. Each one worked for a while. At some point I would start to feel deprived and left out of the fun that I imagined other people were having while they were eating food that I wasn't allowed to eat. I wasn't the least bit interested in learning to be disciplined—I just wanted to eat with abandon. So I would binge and easily find all the weight that I had lost.

I was determined to figure out what was wrong with me. Why did I have this obsession with food? Why couldn't I learn self-control? Why did I hate myself so much that I made myself fat? I believed that if I was "overweight" that it was a sign of there being something wrong with me.

I focused my attention fully on the fascinating area of self-help books. There are thousands of them! All the best books will tell you exactly what is wrong with you and what you have to change about yourself in order to be happy. And if you follow their instructions you will finally be OK.

I spent years trying to follow system after system wondering what was wrong with me and why those books hadn't fixed me yet. Each one had me focus on my faults and each one just did not feel right. I changed my behavior and still felt bad so I would try another book.

One day I had a moment of insight that took me in a completely new and different direction. I was standing in front of my mirror getting ready for a New York City night on the town with some girlfriends and I realized that the thought going round and round was "you're too fat to be pretty." I was shocked when I heard it. Did that come from me? I was looking at my reflection and truth be told, I thought I looked pretty darn good. Why should I have to wait to love myself until I look physically different? Besides, body image is something that changes with every society and culture, and even decade by decade. There was a time when a Rubenesque figure was the ideal.

I began to consider that how I felt about food was how I felt about my life. When I felt that I wanted to eat with abandon—what I really wanted was to live with abandon. I wanted to live without restraint. I wanted to live fully and outrageously without the burden of negative self-judgment. I wanted to feel like I had a right to pursue every dream and have it all—and I didn't want to work hard to feel that way. I wanted it to be fun.

I am now determined that every day I will laugh, that I will eat food that tastes good without feeling guilty and that I will look at myself in a mirror with approval.

I created www.ThisLushLife.com as my way to remind myself every day that life is good, that I am beautiful at any size, and that the source of my beauty comes from living a pleasurable life. I want women to be able to shop in a size-positive environment where we will never post diet ads.

ThisLushLife.com is a website where women can shop for clothing, make travel plans, decorate their homes, send flowers and purchase gifts without being harassed by images of someone else's physical ideal. In our plus-size clothing section we will only represent websites that use plus-size models. We want every visitor to feel a sense of self-approval and enjoy this lush life that we are all blessed to be living.

"Live the Life you Love and Love the Life you Live."

LESLEIGH J. OWEN

I truly, deeply, authentically believe that fat is beautiful. I find rolls, bulges, teddy-bear tummies, squishy and dimpled thighs, softly padded knees, delicately draped ankles, undulating bee-hinds, and shining, round faces to be more beautiful and grabbable than anything I've seen slither out of Hollywood. Fat people are parades of tactile sensation: warm, soft, and giving. I find a particular kind of beauty and strength in fat people that I just don't find anywhere else.

Excerpt from a letter I wrote to Fat Poets' Society members in fall 2006—

My beautiful, beloved mother tells me my first feat of activism came about at the tender age of three. While shopping for dolls (or cupcakes, or coloring books), she tells me, I would always grab the broken, misshapen, or less popular ones. When she would ask me why, I would adamantly reply, "I saved them from being sad because no one else would buy them!" I like to picture that round-cheeked, fat little girl, hands on hips, Mary Janes defiantly outturned, imaginary cape billowing as she championed all oppressed pastries and plastic playthings.

Thirty years later, I would like to think my life has done justice to that dark-haired little girl. I'm now a Ph.D. candidate in sociology, a college instructor, and a social activist, working to address inequalities, challenge people to think critically, and—ah, heck, let's face it—to make the world a better place.

My activism career per se (i.e., involving people rather than stuffed animals) began in my teens. Marching in parades, participating in letter writing campaigns, and rallying in front of governmental buildings seemed like the perfect match for my crazy combination of idealism, passion, and, truthfully, a shameless love of drama and theater. Naturally, I couldn't wait for college.

I started college in my home state of Idaho as a vocal performance major, but within a year switched to the social sciences. The next few years were hectic, stressful, and incredibly empowering; feminist activism became my lighthouse in an endless, choppy sea of full-time jobs and heavy course loads.

By my mid-20s I was involved in countless progressive organizations, but, like many of the feminists writing in *Shadow on a Tightrope,* the germinal fat pride collection of essays and poetry, I felt devalued and misunderstood as a fat feminist. My personal and political focuses have shifted since then to include progressive movements and the body, especially in terms of fatness, sexuality, and beauty. Instead of protecting the "ugly," the unwanted, and the devalued, I became interested in constructing new, more comprehensive, definitions of beauty and worth.

I earned my B.S. degree (no comment) in social sciences in the late 1990s. In the interest of earning my doctorate in sociology and eventually becoming a college professor, I reluctantly relocated to California at the tender age of 27 to attend graduate school. I am currently living in L.A. County in California, writing my dissertation on fat folks, including how we experience our fatness, what it means to us, and how it shapes our understandings of ourselves as beautiful women and men.

Right now, 32 years old, married, taking a year off from teaching in order to write my dissertation, owned by three cats, heavily enmeshed in fat pride activism, I couldn't be happier. Well, the American political climate could use a little tweak here and there, and okay, maybe the environment isn't doing so well. And sure, maybe the world isn't the exact one three-year-old me would have created, but that's why we have dedicated and beautiful folks like the ones in the Fat Poets' Society.

The world may not be a perfect place, but I like to think we activists are shaping it into a better, more inclusive, one.

FRANNIE ZELLMAN

All my life it seemed strange to me that I was stigmatized and ostracized for something that didn't seem to be hurting anyone—i.e., that I happened to be fat. Since I could walk slimmer friends into the ground, I knew that my being fat had little or no bearing on my health.

So what was it that people were so angry about, I wondered? I didn't murder people or hurt anyone deliberately. I tried to pursue my hobbies, earn a living, have fun with friends. What was so terrible about being fat?

The answer only came to me years later, after I had joined NAAFA—the National Association to Advance Fat Acceptance—and read a wonderful magazine called *Radiance* and talked with other fat people: Nothing.

Fat people have the same thoughts, concerns, dreads, joys, dreams and hopes that slimmer people do. Which is good, I guess, since we number more than half the population, according to numerous health agencies and groups. So I am a member of a majority—a majority that is only starting to realize how it has been tyrannized and demonized by a not-very-well meaning minority. I am still waiting for the fat revolution.

Anyone who really appreciates fat people knows that the only thing we "need" is to be left to lead our lives happily and peacefully without hatred, prejudice or discrimination, and with access to the same opportunities for jobs, education, housing and health benefits that exist for slimmer people.

I come from politically active and involved individuals on both sides of my family. Unfortunately, people who concern themselves with issues of the day and with making sure that other ostracized groups gain access to power circles, decision-making and cultural legitimacy have really dragged their feet when it comes to standing with fat people as we go up against the Medical Establishment, the Health Establishment, the Pharmaceutical Establishment and cultural and fashion institutions everywhere.

What we don't need is to be told time and time again that we should lose weight. Not only does dieting not lead to losing weight, but it is time that people started to see that beauty and health are not the sole province of people who can fit under beds easily.

Being fat is a major part of my identity, but previously I wrote around it as if it—and in large part (pun intended) I myself—didn't exist. To write and acknowledge and even celebrate myself as a fat poet is soul-satisfying beyond words and beyond relief.

ABOUT PEARLSONG PRESS

Pearlsong Press is an independent publishing company dedicated to providing books and resources that entertain while expanding perspectives on the self and the world. The company was founded by Peggy Elam, Ph.D., a psychologist and journalist, in 2003.

Pearls are formed when a piece of sand or grit or other abrasive, annoying, or even dangerous substance enters an oyster and triggers its protective response. The substance is coated with shimmering opalescent nacre ("mother of pearl"), the coats eventually building up to produce a beautiful gem. The self-healing response of the oyster thus transforms suffering into a thing of beauty.

The pearl-creating process reflects our company's desire to move outside a pathological or "disease" based model into a more integrative and transcendent perspective on life, health, and well-being. A move out of suffering into joy. And that, we think, is something to sing about.

Pearlsong Press endorses **Health At Every Size**, an approach to health and well-being that celebrates natural diversity in body size and encourages people to stop focusing on weight (or any external measurement) in favor of listening to and respecting natural appetites for food, drink, sleep, rest, movement, and recreation. While not every book we publish specifically promotes Health At Every Size, none of our books or other resources will contradict this holistic and body-positive perspective.

We encourage you to **enjoy, enlarge, enlighten and enliven yourself** with other Pearlsong Press books, including:

FatLand: a novel by Frannie Zellman

Measure by Measure
a novel by Rebecca Fox & William Sherman

10 Steps to Loving Your Body
(No Matter What Size You Are)
self-help & inspiration by Pat Ballard

The Program
a novel by Charlie Lovett

Off Kilter: A Woman's Journey to Peace
with Scoliosis, Her Mother, & Her Polish Heritage
a memoir by Linda C. Wisniewski

Splendid Seniors: Great Lives, Great Deeds
by Jack Adler

The Singing of Swans
a novel about the Divine Feminine
by Mary Saracino

Beyond Measure:
A Memoir About Short Stature & Inner Growth
by Ellen Frankel

Unconventional Means:
The Dream Down Under
a memoir by Anne Richardson Williams

Taking Up Space
a sociological memoir by Pattie Thomas, Ph.D.
with Carl Wilkerson, M.B.A.
(foreword by Paul Campos,
author of *The Obesity Myth*)

Romance novels and short stories
featuring Big Beautiful Heroines
by Pat Ballard, the Queen of Rubenesque Romances:

The Best Man	*Abigail's Revenge*
Dangerous Curves Ahead	*Wanted: One Groom*
Nobody's Perfect	*His Brother's Child*

A Worthy Heir

& Judy Bagshaw:

At Long Last, Love: A Collection

www.ingramcontent.com/pod-product-compliance
Lightning Source LLC
Chambersburg PA
CBHW030013110426
42741CB00032B/543